A Story Unfinished

Alana Varney

BookLeaf Publishing

Presentation by *BookLeaf Publishing*

Web: www.bookleafpub.com

E-mail: info@bookleafpub.com

ISBN: 978-93-95890-31-1

First edition 2022

DEDICATION

To the teachers, writers, singers, and story tellers

Madeline Pandolfi and all the people she's been,

Jason Varney, the young man who dried my tears and my best friend

Aleric, Audrey, and Aries... for everything you are and everything you've turned me into

To my Sister, Gail, Mother of Warriors and my first writing teacher

ACKNOWLEDGEMENT

When I was 13, my family lived in Germany and my sister and I found ourselves doing homeschool, back before computers were in every household and most people had never heard of the internet. Our school was done in paper workbooks, graded by the "home teacher" and sent to the school for grading. The workload wasn't hard, answer keys to "check our work" were plentiful, and most days we were done with whatever assignments we would have been working on early.

On those days, for a brief moment, we were stuck at a large wooden table in a seldom used dining room, lest my mom came home to check on us and found us distracted by a new Nintendo NES.

On those days it was just the two of us, but unlike so many times before, we were together, not in our own corners or rooms or lives.

On those days, we would get distracted, as young kids do, and we would spend time making up rhymes and poetry and fortune cookie sayings, trying to see who could come up with the most profound or funniest or most moving or the most unexpected. It was in this room, in this house, that I think I spent the most time with her; It is where we first watched the Lion King together and where we would play video games, or fight over whose turn it was; it is where I fell in love with words and poetry; it's where we argued over whether songs had words and where she told me, years later, that she was going to have a baby. It is the room where I watched her become a mom, as the table was eventually replaced by a crib.

Homeschool was replaced with jobs and friends and moving on.

We haven't always had the easiest relationship but we have always stayed within the periphery of each other. Even when things were strained and I wasn't sure she liked me, I have never doubted she loves me, and fiercely. And if she doesn't always believe I love her, I always know and sometimes that has to be enough.

Without her influence, her time, and those days stuck together, I don't know who I would be but I know I am better because of those days. I know her constant companionship through childhood created a safety and security in the world that I was able to take for granted in ways that were robbed from her. Because of her, I never felt alone.

PREFACE

I started this project in order to see if I could do it. If you are reading this, that means I did it. While I am hopeful that someone out there will find something in these pages helpful or touching, I wrote this book with the full acknowledgement that it may be the only one I ever write. There are people and thoughts that I had to focus on, the things most important to leave behind, if this is indeed my one shot.

My mother, the beginning of me,
My children, the end of me,
and My wonderful husband who had helped me to find my way to the best places.

This project also taught me that life as a writer is a painful one that doesn't stop when the lines come or when the story is finished. Opening oneself up to the places where all of our best treasures and memories are stored, also creates a vulnerability that can be reactive. Bless the families of the writers and story tellers and singers.

Growth

I

There are times to live life to its fullest,
and times there is barely a spark.
For that which we plant in the daylight,
needs time to take root in the dark.

II

When the world is pressing and changing
and asking us to change, too,
Like a butterfly in a catalyst,
sometimes we feel like goo.

We feel broken and weary, and totally empty,
like we have nothing else to give.
Its not so much that we want to die
but we feel like its too hard to live.

Then piece by piece, we rebuild,
from the things that matter inside
We go through the motions, start to refocus,
and let old habits fall aside.

And then one day from the darkness,
We wake to a world that is new;
Not because of the state that the world is in,
But because of the the things we've been
through.

We find that we've changed...and we haven't;
We've really been Here all along.
But now, somehow... we are different, too;
and our soundtrack holds more songs.

And the things that we love are different;
And the things we love are the same.
And we look to the future with kindness,
instead of the past in shame.

We approach new adventures with gusto;
make plans for our future and then...
Life wears us thin, it happens again,
For Change is the Blessing of Men.

Again, the Darkness, it finds us,
and again, the cycle will start.
We expand and contract, and give birth to that
which we tended and fed in the dark.

So is the nature of growth,
So is the changing tide.
And the one thing that binds us, should always
unite us,
Is the insistent March of Time.

III

So be mindful of what you tend to in darkness,
for everything comes from a seed;
And who we become depends on
whether we rebuild from Love, Hope, or Greed.

Remembering

I am remembering what it is like to be beautiful

So long was I the

worker
the soldier
the exit strategy

Now I am remembering what it is like

to be wanted
to be desired
to be woman
to be mother
to be goddess

I am learning to love my body in a way that
every woman should

the curves, the lines, the wrinkles

the proof of the babies my body has borne,
birthed and nursed.

The scars that tell the stories and the parts that refuse to be tamed.

I am loving myself in a way that I pray my daughters will.

Proud to be woman
to be female
to be here

I am casting off the burdens placed on me by preachers and critics
casting off the unfounded shame of over oppressing religions
casting off an untrue legacy of sin and ruin and shame

I am taking my place among the stars
among the gods
among the goddesses

Feminine

I am a girl. A woman.

A creature of breast and bone and heart.
Perfumed scents and skirt. Lips and hips and curves. I am moody and monthly. I follow moon cycles like my body was connected to the tides; like I was made of water.

Internal ocean.

I am constant thought, opened mouthed and rarely silent.
I am hard to please and unpredictable.
I am face powder and nail polish with lipstick hugging teeth; smeared mascara with baby spit somewhere on my body. The blame of sin carried by my gender for 2000 years weighing heavy on my back, bends me, bends me, bends me, I don't break. I am cleaner, cook, lover, mother, grandmother in waiting, driver, dancer, singer, swimmer, lover, sister, friend. I am woman.

Feminine

More than music

I

He walks in musical tones
like his body was the instrument,
his feet stepping to drum beats;
Sometimes quick-footed, Allegro in action,
Other times, he is Adagio, his footsteps falling
like a funeral march.

He is a full orchestra unto himself
arms conducting,
mind racing,
as this world falls away and he creates a world
around him full of symphony and song,
constantly writing his life's melody out of strings
and dreams.

and for a moment, this mythical man walking
into adulthood, is 5 years old, holding a violin
that is slightly too big for his small hands, trying
to stretch his pinky, and Ms. Bass is telling him
to
"Reach"

II

She is stories and imagination; fearlessness and strength.
She is hope and friendships and power ballads.
She is loyal to those she loves; protector of others; learning to protect herself.
She is stress and worry, and way too hard on herself.

She is listener
- negotiator
- story weaver
- and loved.

Containing galaxies within her center, tempering waves that rise to meet her, she is song, and voice, and projection.

She hides daggers in her fingertips and can make the deepest cuts; she is Justice
and she welcomes the ground beneath her feet, as an old friend, full of self and kinship.

Now, on the edge of freedom, with life's longing reaching out to grasp her, I can see the hunger in her eyes.

and for a moment she is 8 years old, looking for me in the first row of her music recital, and I hear Ms. Bass whispering,

"Just Breathe"

III

They are fire, bright and burning; protection and light.
Forged from stardust and love overflowing
balance
chaos
change

Commander of the room, changing moods with their walk, forcing the ground to give way beneath their feet.

Able to find the most shadowed recesses of their room, their world, their selves...an invisibility spell that is quickly wearing off as they begin to show up and take their place in the world.

As they emerge, I see characters and choices and brilliance stitched together with persistence and self determination; More than anyone else they are the embodiment of all of us, born into love and friendship and family.

They are eyerolls and attitude
- goodness and adventure
- anger and remorse
- gratitude and forgiveness
- connections and bonds

They are unsure and brave and willing to try new things. They are recipes and history and so much like their father. And, as I watch them leave the darkness of their magnificent transformation,

this perpetually burning Pheonix is 10 years old, nervously shuffling in front of the microphone, and Ms. Bass is reminding them,

"You got this!"

Mr. Mean Candy Corn

The last night of the fair, and there on the grounds,
was a family of 5, trudging around.

The weather had turned, the hour was late,
So the family decided to head for the gate.

But on the way out, the youngest on squealed,
"There is one more game open! 'Just Spin the Wheel'".

She pleaded and pleaded, and then begged some more,
"Can I PLEASE try ONE time, for the pink unicorn?"

Her father relented, her siblings both groaned;
Cold, tired, and wet, they wished to be home.

But the decision was made so the kid got her shot,
She spun the wheel hard, and then hoped a LOT.

As the wheel slowed, the girl's eyes got bright,
as the pink unicorn square came into sight.

Slower and slower, the wheel creaked along,
She KNEW she would win! She couldn't be wrong!

As the final clicks of wheel made their sound,
The unicorn picture had made it's way round!

And then, just like that! The wheel clicked once more,
and all of her hopes crashed on tent floor.

She looked at the board, tears filling her eyes,
As the wheel finally stopped, to reveal her new prize.

And there on the board was a picture so worn,
She could hardly make out the small candy corn.

The Brother and Sister began to laugh,
as the Little One's hopes were utterly dashed.

And the carnival man pulled down from the rack
a small little candy corn stuffed in the back.

He offered the toy to the little girl there,
But she refused to take it, and she started to wail.

The mom took the toy and thanked the kind man,
then escorted the family to the old minivan.

The Brother and Sister begged for the plush
and the Little One said she "didn't care...much."

So the Daddy relented and passed on the toy,
he handed the candy corn to his only boy.

And the Brother began, like big brothers do,
to tease his small sister, and make voices, too.

"I am Mr. Candy Corn," the Brother said with doom.
"And I will be coming for you!" he added with extra gloom.

Then Sister grabbed the toy and screeched, "No! you got it wrong!"
She drew an X on his eye as she sang a song:

~ I am Mr. Mean Candy Corn
and this is what I see,
Everywhere that I am at,
That's where Mischief Be! ~

And the kids laughed and laughed, because they did not know,
A spell was cast, the moment that, those simple words were spoke.

They did not know, they did not care, the moon was full that day.
The Solstice Magic was afoot... and Magic finds a way.

And just like that, they all moved on, having quickly gotten bored.
And Mr. Mean Candy corn was discarded to the floor.

As the night wore on and the family neared home, the children fell asleep,
until the tire went flat; A BOOM, A SPLAT! They were awakened from the deep.

But Daddy changed the tire, and soon they were home again,
and gathering all of that day's goods, Mom took Mr. Mean Candy Corn in.

But nobody liked him. And nobody cared
about the stuffed candy corn they got at the fair.

So nobody noticed, and nobody guessed,
when Mr. Mean Candy Corn was found near a mess,

That the Mischief afoot was born on the night
When the Little One's tears fell in the Solstice moonlight.

They didn't notice when he was found on the floor,
his short little arm caught in the fridge door;
The Little One was blamed for the food that spoiled,
for leaving her toys on a floor that was soiled.

They didn't notice, and they couldn't tell,
when Sister slipped in the water, he was right near the pail.

And they didn't notice when he was found
near Brother's computer that didn't shut down;
They didn't notice when the fire was out
that Mr. Mean Candy Corn was sitting about.

And all through the years, no one noticed or guessed, that so much that had went awry,
Was due to some words, a stuffed candy corn, a full moon, and a late Solstice night.

Wherever Chaos and Disorder were found, Mr. Mean Candy Corn was always nearby, with his small little arms, and his small little legs, and black X over his right eye.

~ I am Mr. Mean Candy Corn
and this is what I see,
Everywhere that I am at,
That's where Mischief Be! ~

Masculine

I gave him a baby bluebird, fallen out of a nest
and he held it, tried to feed it, and sat with it.
He mourned it when it died.
It was the most masculine thing I have ever
seen.

Reminiscing

The little leaf never knew how much it contributed to the the Tree of Life, until it fell away, and saw the whole picture. -Madeline Pandolfi, philosopher

Goodnight kisses and Christmas mornings,
laundry mats and laughter,
these are the things I think about
when I think about my mother.

Long walks around the lake
Cinnamon rolls and strength
Hugs and wishes , washing dishes
and all the little things.

Beaches in the summer, costumes in the fall,
a love of travel, knowing what matters,
From her, I got it all.

Forgiveness and intention, and learning how to breathe,
These are just some of the priceless gifts she bestowed on me.

Reading poetry in the living room and getting dizzy at the fair,
Amongst my most treasured memories, she is always there.

From her I learned what love is
and how to hold a child
how to watch your baby leave and somehow force a smile.

She taught me how to be selfless
and how to speak out loud
and she is the reason I've become
The person I am now.

I see her in my children
I know her in bones
I know she will ALWAYS be with me
No matter where she goes.

In a Gereration

That's just the way it is; Ah, but don't you believe them- Bruce Hornsby

My grandmother wasn't allowed to have her own bank account, until my mom was 3.

My mother was 14 before birth control became accessible and she was 16 when before the grand courts determined that women were, in fact, capable of functioning while pregnant.

and I.... I was

1 years old before a woman was ever placed on the Supreme Court
1 - before Columbia University allowed women to attend.
4 - when the first woman was nominated by a major party for Vice President
14 - when it was decided that girls should be given equal opportunities in math and science
17 - when they decided to fund women's college athletics

17 -when the first female Secretary of State was appointed
25 - when I witnessed the 4th woman and First Hispanic American woman to serve on the Supreme Court
27 -when I watched the First female Speaker of the House be sworn in
30 - when Terri A Sewell became the First Black woman to represent Alabama in the United States House of Representatives.
33- Before women were deemed "fit for combat"
41 -When I witness the election of the first female Vice President of the United States of America
41 -When the first female Secretary of the United States Army was appointed

I am 42.

One generation.

100 years from the right to vote
Over 50% bachelor's degrees going to women since 1980 (year BEFORE Columbia allowed women)
Less than 10 years from "fit for combat" to Head of the Army

curiosity

It's not that death's bad
But I would live forever
...see what happens next

Father

From the first man I called father,
I got my blood and bones;
- a broken man who made me understand that
men
speak in "deep tones."
He showed me how he could strike fear in his
little pet,
By talking very angrily, by yelling, or with a hit.
He taught me men were better and women
should submit,
His carelessness and selfishness taught me,
"Men don't give a shit."

The second person I called father,
I met when I was five.
He taught me that men were loud
and unhappy with their lives.
He taught me men don't like dogs
or enjoy the family strain
and that men find the most happiness in the old,
fermented grain.
His trauma taught me silence;
His rage it taught me well,
that men do not deal in feelings
they're just suffering through Hell.

The third man I called father
I met when I was young,
And this amazing man taught me,
the other two were wrong.
He taught me men can love life, even when its tough;
and men can do the work they need, even when it's rough.
And men can find the trauma, and men can heal their pain,
and men can find the softest touch, as gentle as the rain.
He also taught me quickly, that a man can be a steady shore,
a guiding light, a place to fall, a friend, and so much more.

He taught me men can love someone, deeper than the sea
and he showed me how a loving touch defines Masculinity.
He taught me that real leaders, lead by going through,
Not by shouting orders, telling others what to do.
He taught me men can provide a cozy place of rest,
a safe space, a warm embrace, a place to lay your head.

He showed me men can love
the family they create,
princess crowns, the soccer rounds,
the recitals and the plays.

He showed men are open, loving, strong and
warm, and I wish that I had known that from the
moment I was born.

But life is what we make it and a little what we
got,
So when I saw this soul of a man, I cast in my
lot.
And I took this young and wizened man,
and swore to be his friend;
we were wed, and as I've said,
the story doesn't end.

For in his wake he has replaced every doubt and
fear I had,
and I know that now my son will be a caring,
loving dad.
And my daughters were born to someone, who
always knew their worth,
to a father's love, a strong man's hugs, the man
who loved them first.

Him

He loves me like it's easy
  Like I am not made of turbulent seas...
    or, rather, like he likes to ride the waves.

He loves me like he will miss
my constant scattered messes,
my unexpected less
my days of feeling fed up with the world
and my unrelenting optimism that, somehow,
everything will be ok.

He loves me like I'm magic.
Like I can make everything ok.

He loves me like he was made for me
    like he stitched himself together, just for me,
out of ambition and dreams
and his longing to love me.

I love him like there are no words
  Like time has no meaning
  Like forever would never be long enough
  Like he created the best parts of me
  Like everything else was just waiting, just
practice, just passing time

Like there is more of me with him than before him

Like we are decades, like we are eternal, like we will never die.

Writing

This is how we process
in metaphors and contradictions;
The beautiful expanse of light;
The never ending darkness.

Tragedies beget heroes
Love stories beget ballads
Anger begets demons
and hope begets forgiveness and triumph

Lives rising and falling
worlds spun out of imagination, anguish, and joy

Pain giving way to joy
stories with happy endings
and stories that just end

a page, a little ink:
creation manifest

Writers have an alchemy,
transforming time, space, and tragedy
into something we can hold

Made of Stardust

Will we ever learn our lesson,
Will we ever finally see,
that humanity is made for more
than to satisfy one's greed?

We are made for moments;
for laughing, love, and more...
Seeking out connections
from the moment we are born.

We are hopes and dreams and travel,
loss and failure, too;
try again, start afresh,
becoming someone new.

We are made of consequence, ancestors stitched
through time
And death will come upon us; we're just one
more in the line.
And all the gold and riches, and all the stock
bonds too,
are nothing but mere illusions, distracting us
from truth.

We are people breathing, dying at it's best,
it's not what we take that matters, but what we leave the rest.
A dragon's horde can't save you, for death's always at the door
but caring about each other, is what we are made for.

Heaven and Hell

What is Hell but loneliness?
- emptiness, and grief?
- a life of struggle, no help in sight,
- no moment of relief.

What is Heaven, but connection?
- community and love?
- a moment of faith, a still, saving grace
- knowing we're all good enough.

What is Hell, but a landscape?
- a desolate, fiery scene?
- Where the earth is all scorched,
the hungry ignored, and things are just what
they seem?

What is Heaven but a Paradise?
- a place where everyone's free?
- to rejoice and give thanks
for the things that we take
and celebrate all that we see.

What is Hell but anguish?
What is Hell but pain?
What is Heaven but a holy place
where everyone fits in?

What if Heaven isn't "up there"
and Hell is no distant place?
What if Earth is something we construct,
by the choices that we make?

Middle School is the Hardest

At 11:
My child seems sad all the time and doesn't want to talk.
They have gotten moody and there's anger in their walk.

At 12:
My child rolls their eyes and doesn't like the chores,
they only want to "do what they want" and they're breaking all the norms.

At 13:
My child is hidden and distant,
locked in their room all the time.
When I ask them small questions,
they act like I've lost my mind.

I tell them it's all developmental,
and they look at me in shock,
How could such disrespect be expected,
and then they give me "that look".

That look that tells what they're thinking,
they think that I've gone mad.
I must not understand their case,
the child's attitude is BAD!

I take a deep breath and tell them,
This is something that comes with time.
As kids grow up, they get ideas,
and start to wonder why.

A time comes when one day a baby... kid... a child,
wakes up with brand new skills and lots of thoughts to try.

For the first time they can feel anger,
in a way they never could before,
and the chemical rush, comes in like a gush,
in ways they can't ignore.

They make friends and it seems just like magic,
emotions become magical too
music and dance and ideas of romance all begin to take bloom.

And the rush of excitement or danger, or
frustration or sadness, or grief
overwhelm the most respectful child,
and the huffing gives them relief.

And its not enough for some parents,
that the child takes out the trash,
they prefer that the kid does it with happiness,
forethought, and dash.

But the child is not being hurtful,
it is just that they don't yet know how,
to speak respectfully angry, notice their grumpy,
or even how to calm down.

Overwhelmed and untrained, they are anxious,
and they really don't know what to do
But they will learn to control it,
it takes more than a moment,
remember back when they were 2?

Reteach them to use their words wisely,
how to identify feelings and then
Remind them you love them,
squeeze them and hug them,
and let them try again.

Every feeling doesn't need to be punished,
every sigh doesn't mean they are bad,
They are just starting to learn to be human,
the beautiful, the ugly, the sad.
The feelings can shatter and stagger,
as childhood fantasies fall.
I promise it is not just your child,

it happens to them all.
Remind them that taking a breath is better,
than lashing out and causing a scene,
that anger can find us any time but it's our
choice to let it reign

And I remind the parents it's normal,
they are doing a good job indeed,
but we are all growing up and it doesn't matter if
we are 30 or 13
we all have room for improvement,
we all seem frustrated when mad
but adults have to learn how to make room for a
child's happy, anxious, and sad.

I also gently remind them,
that are not alone,
kids are known for being jerks,
and the kids will soon be grown.

The Miner

My father told me once,
when I was just a child
that back in his younger days,
he used to be a Miner.

I thought about him getting up
Before the rising sun,
Strapping up his steel-toed boots
Before the day begun.

I imagined him at work
hard hat on his head,
Everything he went through
to keep his family fed.

I thought about the times,
he spent beneath the ground,
digging up the minerals
and treasures to be found.

I thought about the birds
that may have gave their lives
so that my father could stay safe
and make it home alive.

I thought about the danger
and how hard must be the life
For those who are a Miner
and make such sacrifice.

One day I asked my older brother,
to see just what he'd say,
Of what he did remember of
my Father's mining days.

He took a breath and waited,
like he didn't know what to say;
And then he told me something,
that changed the way I think.

He told that our father
did not suffer much,
he did not work in filth or grime,
or anything as such.

He told me that our father
never worked in muck,
My father was a SALT MINER,
and drove a fancy truck.

Choosing disbelief

Some people are born with tails, or extra arms or webbed feet.
Some people are born with less chromosomes than average and some people have a little extra in the mix.

People are born different colors than their parents, due to how our ancestors keep showing back up.
Sometimes the heart, the bone, the lip doesn't fuse right.
Sometimes, what was once a hope of a baby, doesn't make it because vital pieces never develop.
Sometimes twins are co-joined and sometimes people are born with the ability to recreate a skyline after just one brief look.
Some people are born seeing music, and some people are born color blind. Some people are born with no depth perception and some people are not able to see.
Some people are tall, some short, some naturally calm, and others who seem to come into the world ready to fight for something.

A multitude of different skin tones, hair colors, eyes.
People born with freckles, different blood types; people who never get sick and people who have asthma, lungs always in protest.
A spectacular range of human expression and experience.

And, despite all the obvious, miraculous, fantastical expressions that make up the human race, I find it really odd, that some people find it easy to believe a person can be born without organs or allergic to dust, but have a hard time believing not everyone is straight.

Tomorrow

I have a hard relationship with Hope. A constant companion, I usually welcome the company, the daydream, the wish for the great, "One day..." But lately, in the face of a falling world, I seem to be at odds with Hope.

I find the persistent, "just keep going" mantra of Hope annoying and pesky, like mosquitos that always remind you they are there, no matter how unwanted, no matter how much you push them away.

I am tired of Hope's silent waiting,
presumptuous and arrogant;
ignoring my efforts to banish, insisting I am just throwing a fit, just having a tantrum, just getting it out of my system.

I am tired of Hope's whispered, reaching, melodies of how great the world can be. Tired of the songs of better days, unrelenting spirits, and happy times ahead.

I am tired of holding this candle.
I am tired of being a light.
I am tired of "what is possible"

I am tired of Hope's nonchalance, feeling comfortable in any room,
unfazed by time and circumstance.
I am tired of Hope's relaxed posture, no tension in the bones,
no signs of wear.

I am tired of marching.
I am tired of writing.
I am tired of waiting.
I am tired of watching other light-bearers fall.

I am tired of Hope's mocking tone asking if I am ready to give up?
Asking me if being tired is good enough?
  A good enough reason to quit?
  A good enough to reason to stop?
  A good enough reason to leave the world to those who spread decay?

I am tired of going to sleep, thinking tomorrow will be better, and waking up to more hurt, and hunger, and disease playing out on the world stage.

I am tired of Hope asking me, "what can we do in this moment?"

Asking me how I can make one more thing better;

As if this little piece of earth, like my little piece of life, could ever change the state of the world or make the great, "One day..." come.

I am tired of Hope laughing when I say we need to take a break, that I need some time. Laughing like they think I would be lost without them, like a loving parent laughs at a small, tired child who is too tired to calm down.

I am tired of Hope refusing to leave, unwelcomed and unwanted.

I am tired of Hope sending me happy thoughts, and dreams of when, and wrapping me in blankets when I just want to be cold.

I am tired of Hope smiling at me with compassion, telling me things will be ok... reminding me that in order to be done, all I have to do is quit.

I am tired of Hope giving me glimpses of the other light-bearers in the world, letting their

light reach into my darkness, asking me if I am
ready to leave them one man down.

I am tired of hoping sitting with me as history
washes over me, the past, the present, and what
was in-between. Reminding me that growing
pains are not just for muscles, not just for
adolescence, not just for individuals.

I am tired of Hope fawning over the small
progresses, pointing back to the all the small
progresses made, reminding me that the only
way to change is slowly and then all at once.

I am just tired. So I sit, and I listen to Jewel;
I think of my hands.
I think of how growing feels like breaking...
I will not be made useless
I won't be idled with despair
I think of waste and worry and uselessness.

And I pray

And I remember we are creators
And Hope, intrusively emerges, singing a song
of rejoicing,,
rhyming in riddles and asking me what kind of
future am I going
to create?

And I send them to a long forgotten guest room, letting them stay just one more night; waiting one more day before I decide to throw the towel in.

I listen to Billy Joel
sing me to sleep
with the promises of what can be,
after two-thousand years.

And I rest.

The hard things

I thought writing would be easy,
just like I used to do...
That the words would flow,
the feelings show
and I would hear the Muse.

But that isn't quite what happened,
I found a deeper truth,
the words weren't hard,
I found the Bard,
It's what those words led to.

Sitting with my feelings,
turning them to rhyme,
cuts a deeper path
than I expected at the time.

The hard part isn't words,
or printing things to page,
its tears that fall,
the tender call,
and feeling all the rage.

The hard part is in feeling,
each and every line

then going home,
being done,
and acting like your fine.

My feelings rose to surface
my patience, it wore thin
My voice got loud,
I was not proud,
I couldn't keep it in.

The hard part is in feeling,
at the end of each hard line,
the exquisite, sad
the happy, mad
and then leaving it behind.

It is hard when you carry with you
the wounds you choose to share;
poetry or art
music or heart,
the proof of a soul made bare.

What We Inherit

My ancestors who walked before, gave me
blood and bone: A lineage of other people's
footpaths. A mix of traits: height, eye color, and
a doorway to come through.

But, my ancestors are not my heritage.

My heritage is born by those whose mantle I
have tried to pick up, unfinished goals and
extraordinary dreams.
More than coding, these forbearers gave me
purpose and encouragement.

When the darkest of times fall upon us, the
flickering flame of some genetic connection
does not light the way for the paths that I would
take.
Instead, I run blindly in the direction of the
burning fire;
Across the ambers that continue to boil beneath
the corruption,
continues to destroy that which should fall,
giving light to those around them,
eons after their years have closed.

I follow the light of all those who refused to back down, guiding my path: the Freedom Fighters, those who bore the strain of time, and those who worked for a world that they only lived in faith.

My heritage is Galileo, Seeker of Other Wolds;

Socrates, Corruptor of Youth, Seeker of Truth

Women who wouldn't back down,
the people who wouldn't be silent in the face of evil,
and those who dared to dream bigger.

Though Southern, I am neither confederate nor traitor.
I am not separate fountains or billy clubs.

I am more Rebecca Falton and less those ancient British, who gave my grandfather his name.
I am more Ruth than Grandmother,
more Lewis than Jackson,
more forward than backwards,
more lighting fires and less sizzling out.

I am born of an everlasting battle,
of angels and protectors,
of faith and hope, and something better.

of rage
and change
and love
and all rising together.

I am Destructor of Complacency; my inheritance
one of struggle and fight.

For the blood of a covenant is thicker than the
water of the womb,
and what I pass on to those who come after me,
is less about where I come from, and more about
what I do.

World's Oldest Millenial

I am the world's oldest millennial..

there is supposed to be a grand poem, claiming
the title...

but I am tired.

I'll get back to it later when I am finished raising
children and cleaning up this mess.

www.ingramcontent.com/pod-product-compliance
Lightning Source LLC
Chambersburg PA
CBHW051736130826
49812CB00033B/885